WHY ~~EVERY~~ NEEDS DELIVERANCE

"How To Maintain Your Freedom"

Sherene
Mary Nottage
God loves you
May. 10. 19

MATTIE NOTTAGE
MINISTRIES

Prophetess Dr. Mattie Nottage

WHY EVERYONE NEEDS DELIVERANCE
"How To Maintain Your Freedom"

Published By: Mattie Nottage Ministries, International
ISBN 13: 978-09976007-5-9

P.O. Box SB–52524
Nassau, N. P. Bahamas
Tel: (888) 825-7568 or (242) 698-1383

www.mattienottage.org

Unless otherwise indicated, all Scripture quotations are taken from the King James Version, biblegateway.com and The Amplified Bible ©1987 by the Zondervan Corporation and the Lockman Foundation, Grand Rapids, Michigan.

Cover design by: Beyond All Barriers Publications & Media Group
Edited by: Beyond All Barriers Publications & Media Group
Format and Interior design by: Beyond All Barriers Publications & Media Group

DEDICATION

This book is dedicated to believers all around the world who believe that God wants to deliver and set them totally free from every yoke of the enemy.

It is my earnest prayer that you will allow the Spirit of God to set you free so that you can live the abundant life that He has designed for you. I earnestly pray that this book will lead you on a life-changing spiritual journey towards your deliverance as you cultivate a more intimate relationship with God!

ACKNOWLEDGEMENTS

I honor God, Abba, my Father, who has used the foolish things of the world to confound the wise and counted me worthy to equip, instruct, empower and bring deliverance to the body of Christ through the preached, prophetic and written word of God. Without reservation, He will always be first in my life.

I thank God for my husband, spiritual covering and ministry tag team partner, Apostle Edison Nottage, our children and grandchildren. Their unwavering love, support and motivation inspire me to continue to be an available vessel for the Master's use.

Finally, I thank God for my spiritual sons and daughters around the world who desire to be taught and empowered in the things of God. Your desire for more of God continues to inspire me to pursue Him and unveil a greater revelation of who our God is to the world. Thank you for your undying love and support. God bless you!

TABLE OF CONTENTS

Dedication...iv
Acknowledgements...vi
Table of Contents..viii

CHAPTER ONE...1
THE SUPERNATURAL GOD HAS COME TO DELIVER YOU...............2
DELIVERANCE IS THE CHILDREN'S BREAD 3
SPIRITUAL WARFARE 5
EXPOSING YOUR ADVERSARY 9
THE FATHER OF LIES 12
HOW TO KNOW WHEN YOU NEED DELIVERANCE 15

CHAPTER TWO..21
WHERE DID THIS DEMONIC ATTACK COME FROM 22
WHAT IS A DEMON 24
CLASSIFICATION OF DEMONS 25
DEMONIC INFILTRATION 28
HOW DO DEMONS ENTER..32
DEMONS ENTER THROUGH GATEWAYS TO THE SOUL 33
DEMONS CAN ENTER IN GANGS 40
TIME-RELEASED CURSES 41
DEMONOLOGY AND DREAMS...42
HOW DEMONS MANIPULATE YOUR DREAMS 43
SPIRITUAL GENETIC RE-MODIFICATION OF THE SOUL................47

CHAPTER THREE...51
WHAT IS AN ALTAR 52
DEMONIC ALTARS VS HOLY ALTARS 54
EVERY KINGDOM IS GOVERNED BY AN ALTAR............................58
BEWARE OF THE SPIRIT OF HEROD 59
MESSIAH IS HERE 62

CHAPTER FOUR...66
I AM A CHRISTIAN…WHY DO I NEED DELIVERANCE 68
EXPOSING THE SPIRIT OF WITCHCRAFT 70
WHEN YOU ARE UNDER A WITCHCRAFT ATTACK........................73
WHAT IS A CURSE 76
FROM GENERATION TO GENERATION 81
BLOODLINE CURSES 82
GENERATIONAL CURSES, FAMILIAR, FAMILIAL SPIRITS...................86

TABLE OF CONTENTS CONT'D...

CHAPTER FIVE...89
DELIVERANCE IS ALWAYS NECESSARY 90
DELIVERANCE DESTROYS AFFLCITION 92
THE PROCESS OF DELIVERANCE 94
DELIVERANCE FROM CURSES, SPELLS, FAMILY ALTARS 97
THE PROPHETIC DELIVERER...98
WARNING!!...100
THE MINISTRY OF DELIVERANCE IS A DIVINE CALLING.............101
PRAYER OF DELIVERANCE..102
MAINTAINING YOUR DELIVERANCE.................................106
OVERCOMING DEMONIC SYMPTOMS...............................108
THE PILLARS OF DELIVERANCE..110

CHAPTER SIX 121
ACCESSING THE BLESSINGS OF GOD.................................122
GOD WANTS YOU TO BE SAVED 124
THE ABC'S OF SALVATION 125
DELIVERANCE BY THE LEGAL BLOOD OF JESUS...............126
THE BLOOD SPEAKS..128
DELIVERANCE BY THE NAME OF JESUS..............................129
FREE INDEED 130
SCRIPTURES FOR DELIVERANCE 133

Index 145
Ministry Profile...146

CHAPTER ONE

THE SUPERNATURAL GOD HAS COME TO DELIVER YOU

7And the Lord said, I have surely seen the affliction of my people which are in Egypt, and have heard their cry by reason of their taskmasters; for I know their sorrows;

8And I am come down to deliver them...
(Exodus 3:7-8)

Deliverance is a miraculous gift from God given to His children so that they can live their best life ever! A ***miracle*** is a divine act of God that causes something to manifest that you, in your own human strength, could not cause to happen. A miracle is needed when all of man's efforts have failed and divine intervention from God is badly needed.

Deliverance simply means to be set free from something or someone that once had you in bound or in bondage. The Greek word for deliverance is ***soteria*** (pronounced so-tay-ree'-ah) which means salvation. *Soteria* comes from the root word *Sozo* which means to save or rescue. *Soteria* is further defined as the power of God in demonstration to deliver believers out of the destructive devices of the enemy and into His divine protection.

He that dwelleth in the secret place of the most High shall abide under the shadow of the Almighty. (Psalm 91:1)

DELIVERANCE IS THE CHILDREN'S BREAD

22 And, behold, a woman of Canaan came out of the same coasts, and cried unto him, saying, Have mercy on me, O Lord, thou son of David; my daughter is grievously vexed with a devil.

23 But he answered her not a word. And his disciples came and besought him, saying, Send her away; for she crieth after us.

24 But he answered and said, I am not sent but unto the lost sheep of the house of Israel.

25 Then came she and worshipped him, saying, Lord, help me.

26 But he answered and said, It is not meet to take the children's bread, and to cast it to dogs.

27 And she said, Truth, Lord: yet the dogs eat of the crumbs which fall from their masters' table.

28 Then Jesus answered and said unto her, O
woman, great is thy faith: be it unto thee even
as thou wilt. And her daughter was made
whole from that very hour.
(Matthew 15:22-28)

This Syrophonecian woman was not considered to be a Jew but rather a Samaritan, an ethnic group who were said to be unclean or cursed. However, as a result of her persistent desperation and cry for her daughter, He delivered them. That day her faith had caught Jesus' attention and she received the Children's Bread.

Deliverance is the children's bread; simply meaning that deliverance is a gift from God to His people, the Jews to counteract, overthrow or defeat every device of the enemy. It is a supernatural act of God which removes the yoke of the enemy from your life and sets you totally free.

Thou art the God that doest wonders: thou
hast declared thy strength among the people.
(Psalm 77:14)

As a Christian, you are a part of spiritual Israel, a child of God and entitled to receive the promises and blessings of God which includes deliverance.

It is God's will that His children live life abundantly and to the fullest. As a believer, you are delivered by the faith you have in God. God wants every believer who desires to be all that God has created them to be to embrace the gift of deliverance.

SPIRITUAL WARFARE

Spiritual warfare is an ongoing conflict, struggle or battle that takes place in the realm of the spirit. The "spiritual realm" is a realm that cannot be perceived, handled or manipulated by the natural senses.

In the realm of the spirit, there are two basic kingdoms which exist; the kingdom of darkness and the Kingdom of Light. Each kingdom has a "king" and a domain or domains over which they rule. The kingdom of darkness is controlled by satan, himself while the Kingdom of Light is controlled by Jehovah, God.

Within these realms, each ruling king has legions of angels and other "spiritual authorities" under his command, whose only function is to carry out the orders of the king. In the Kingdom of Light there are holy angels and in the kingdom of darkness there are demons and other wicked spirits.

Each kingdom is strategically set up and has one specific mandate, which is to gain new territories while maintaining ultimate control of territories to which they have already laid claim.

Ultimately, each kingdom is already established in the spiritual realm; the kingdom of darkness operates from the second heaven while the Kingdom of God operates from the third heaven. These realms or spheres of rulership and dominion have already been established.

On earth, however, God has given mankind dominion over all created things. This means that human beings are the only agents authorized to operate in the realm of earth. Therefore, each spiritual kingdom knows that if it is going to advance its agenda in the realm of earth it must take possession of a man or woman through whom it can work.

There is a never-ending war being fought over you in the spiritual realm to determine which of the kingdoms will gain possession, and ultimate control, of your soul. This is the reason why you, as a believer, are engaged in spiritual warfare.

Although God is the Creator and Sovereign Ruler over all things. He created man as a free moral agent with a right to choose. You have the right to decide which kingdom you want to be a part of and who you want to serve.

As the children of Israel were crossing over into a new land they were given the mandate to choose whether they would serve God and live or walk in idolatry and carnal desires; suffering the consequences as a result. Whatever decision they made in their current generation also affected generations to come.

> *15 See, I have set before thee this day life and good, and death and evil;*

> *16 In that I command thee this day to love the LORD thy God, to walk in his ways, and to keep his commandments and his statutes and his judgments, that thou mayest live and multiply: and the LORD thy God shall bless thee in the land whither thou goest to possess it.*

> *17 But if thine heart turn away, so that thou wilt not hear, but shalt be drawn away, and worship other gods, and serve them;*

> *18 I denounce unto you this day, that ye shall surely perish, and that ye shall not prolong your days upon the land, whither thou passest over Jordan to go to possess it.*

> *19 I call heaven and earth to record this day against you, that I have set before you life and*

death, blessing and cursing: therefore choose
life, that both thou and thy seed may live:
(Deuteronomy 30:15–19)

EXPOSING YOUR ADVERSARY
"The Names of Satan"

[9] *And the great dragon was cast out, that old serpent,*
called the Devil, and Satan, which deceiveth the
whole world: he was cast out into the earth, and his
angels were cast out with him.
(Revelation 12:9)

Deliverance comes to the believer in order to set him free from the destructive plans of the enemy for his life. According to *John 10:10*, your adversary, the devil, has one mission, and that is to kill, steal and destroy. Your enemy hates you and will do anything to cause your demise.

He is no respect of persons. He does not care that you are rich or poor; black or white; educated or uneducated; his ultimate goal, mission and aim is to bring people everywhere into bondage.

Genesis 3:15 exposes the eternal hatred that exists between the devil and the "seed of the woman", which represents every human being born:

> *"And I will put enmity between thee and the woman, and between thy seed and her seed; it shall bruise thy head, and thou shalt bruise his heel."*

Enmity means that there is an eternal and irreconcilable hatred between two parties. There will never be peace, but always war. Because you were born, the enemy is going to attack you and seek to oppress you; but be encouraged. God has already set the day and time for you to be set free from every demonic bondage.

Satan is the archenemy of every human being born. Some of the names of satan can be found in *Revelation 12.*

These names also help to describe his function, purpose or characteristics and include, but are not limited to:

- The devil
- The serpent
- The dragon
- The deceiver of the whole earth
- The accuser of the brethren
- Prince of the power of the air
- Father of lies
- Ruler of the kingdom of darkness
- Beelzebub, lord of the flies
- Lucifer, son of the morning

Among his many names, in *Isaiah 14:12-14,* satan is also known as Lucifer. Here we can also see that satan became lifted up in pride and lost his place in heaven and his relationship with God forever.

12 How art thou fallen from heaven, O Lucifer, son of the morning! how art thou cut down to the ground, which didst weaken the nations!

13 For thou hast said in thine heart, I will ascend into heaven, I will exalt my throne above the stars of God: I will sit also upon the mount of the congregation, in the sides of the north:

14 I will ascend above the heights of the clouds; I will be like the most High.
(Isaiah 14:12 – 14)

Satan is also referred to as Beelzebub in **Mark 3:22.** By definition, Beelzebub is a Hebrew name meaning Lord of the flies. It is a name derived from a Philistine god, formerly worshipped in, and later adopted by some religions as a major demon. The name Beelzebub is also associated with the Canaanite god **Baal.**

And the scribes which came down from Jerusalem said, He hath Beelzebub, and by the prince of the devils casteth he out devils. (Mark 3:22)

In **Mark 3:22**, the scribes accused Jesus of driving out demons by the power of Beelzebub, prince of demons, the name also appearing in the expanded version in **Matthew 12:24,27** and **Luke 11:15, 18–19.** The name also occurs in **Matthew 10:25.**

THE FATHER OF LIES

In **John 8:44**, Jesus reveals the devil as the father of lies and a murderer. In **John 10:10** Jesus also exposes your adversary's mission which is to steal, kill and destroy.

> *Ye are of your father the devil, and the lusts of your father ye will do. He was a murderer from the beginning, and abode not in the truth, because there is no truth in him. When he speaketh a lie, he speaketh of his own: for he is a liar, and the father of it.*
> *(John 8:44)*

Two of satan's most effective weapons are deception and lies. He lies to people in order to get them to forfeit the blessings of God for their lives. Just as he deceived Eve in the garden, he continues to deceive people or twist the truth in an effort to get you to doubt God and move away from the things of God.

Similarly, one of his greatest and most deadly deceptive ploys is to try to convince people that he does not exist at all; that there is nothing fighting them and there is no need to be concerned about or engage in any level of spiritual warfare.

This could not be further from the truth. True reality is that whether or not you believe that he exists, he is real; whether you decide to fight or not, he is going to attack you. He is a spiritual principality and your sworn enemy, determined to destroy you and everyone around you.

In order to bring you into bondage, the devil will use various agents from his kingdom of darkness, including but not limited to:
- himself
- principalities, demons and
   powers that dwell in the atmospheric heavens
- evil spirits from the water world also called marine spirits
- a spirit husband or spirit wife
- demons from the regions of hell
- evil spirits that are walking to and fro in the earth

- human spirits of those living or witches through astro-projection
- human spirits of the dead through necromancy

HOW TO KNOW WHEN YOU OR YOUR LOVED ONE NEEDS DELIVERANCE

In many instances, people come seeking deliverance because they believe that their lives or the life of their loved one, is under some form of demonic attack. At times they can recognize that something is wrong but are unable to fully explain what it is.

Severe attacks from the enemy can cause various levels of demonic influence over your life. *To better help you understand, I have divided the realms of demonic influence into three basic levels:*

- ❖ The *first level of demonic influence* can affect you: **TO THE POINT WHERE YOU ARE FULLY AWARE THAT SOMETHING IS WRONG IN YOUR**

LIFE, BUT YOU FEEL AS THOUGH YOU HAVE CONTROL OVER IT and you know within yourself that you need deliverance.

❖ The *second level of demonic influence* may affect your life: **TO THE POINT WHERE YOU ARE AWARE THAT SOMETHING IS WRONG BUT YOU HAVE ABSOLUTELY *NO* CONTROL OVER IT.** However, you know that you need deliverance.

❖ The *third level of demonic influence* in your life can overwhelm you: **TO THE POINT THAT YOU ARE NOT AWARE THAT YOU ARE UNDER A DEMONIC ATTACK AND YOU ARE TOTALLY UNAWARE THAT SOMETHING IS WRONG WITH YOU.** You have no control over this demonic influence and you are in desperate need of total deliverance.

WHY EVERYONE NEEDS DELIVERANCE

You can identify when you or a loved one is under a demonic attack when you experience any of the following, but not limited to:

- You begin to fall out of love with God and lose interest in the things of God.

- You begin to lose your joy and engage in carnal or worldly activities more than you engage in the things of God.

- Your spiritual discernment becomes distorted and you begin to perceive inaccurately; hear incorrectly and interpret wrongly

- You become dysfunctional, confused, easily offended, overly aggressive or abusive

- You begin to suddenly separate yourself from relationships you once valued; for example, a parent, spouse, coach or spiritual leader

- You become tormented for an extended period of time and are unable to sleep throughout the night

- You start hearing voices or experience extreme mind battles.

- You may become extremely stressed out, overly anxious, fearful and insecure.

- You may experience unexplainable and excessive delays, failures and setbacks

- You continually to have contaminated, perverted or evil thoughts.

- You become negative, dismal, overly critical, fault-finding, bitter, resentful, hateful, unforgiving, depressed and even suicidal.

- You experience unusual losses, mishaps, tragedies, traumas and the like.

- You become overtaken in the mental arena and plagued with vexing spirits of depression, discouragement, lows self-esteem or discontentment.

* You become unusually despondent, withdrawn or introverted.

* You develop unexplainable, long-term illnesses or sudden illnesses which the doctors cannot accurately diagnose.

* You begin to experience abnormal swelling in your physical body.

* You begin to feel something moving on the inside of you.

* Your dreams become demonic or perverted. For example, you may see yourself eating something that is contaminated in your dream; you may see yourself being attacked by a spider, snake, dog or other animal. If any of these are appearing in your dream then this means that something distasteful or even reprehensible is taking place. *(See more later in Chapter Two)*

You do not have to live bound by any demonic spirits. God wants you to be totally set free, in Jesus' name.

CHAPTER TWO

WHERE DID THIS DEMONIC ATTACK COME FROM?

The three most important things that an individual needs to identify are the origin, root and source of the attack against his life. Once these are exposed, true deliverance can take place.

There are several basic ways a curse or demonic attack may come to your life and bring you into bondage:

1) Engaging in ungodly or demonic practices, whether knowingly or unknowingly, which may attract demonic oppression to your life; such as consulting with witches, psychics, soothsayers and the like.

2) Evil people who wish to bring hardship or difficulty to your life through rendering curses, spells or evil wishes against your life. These can be spoken or projected as demonic arrows.

3) Demonic spirits can enter your life through your generation line, family

lineage whenever your ancestors worshipped idols or deities. These evil rituals usually involved blood sacrifices of humans or animals. Idolatry grants demons legal rights to afflict or torment anyone within that generational lineage no matter how many decades later.

4) Wicked people may employ the services of a witch or warlock to bring your life into bondage. Once employed, the witch may also utilize familiar spirits to oppress your life. These familiar spirits consult with familial spirits to gain information about your life and your family lineage in order to bring you into bondage.

5) Satan himself, your archenemy, can launch a demonic attack against your life from the realm of darkness. He sends demon spirits to harass and torment your life in order to subvert your divine destiny.

WHAT IS A DEMON?

A *demon* is an evil spirit or personality without a body. Demons work for and with satan to carry out his evil agenda in the earth; to kill, steal from and destroy mankind. Demons seek habitation or a dwelling place which is why they desire to occupy your body. They disturb your life by entering your soul. Once they enter your soul, they overpower your mind, your will, your intellect and or your emotions.

They exist and influence:
- the Marine World
- the Atmosphere World
- the Starry Heavens and the Astral World

Demons do not have legal authority in the earth but they still walk to and fro the earth seeking whom they may devour.

CHARACTERISTICS OF DEMONS

Demons have various function and characteristics by which they tend to operate in order to bind or restrict you. Their primary intention is to infiltrate your life so that you become dysfunctional and miss out on the intended blessings of God.

Some of these characteristics and ways of operating include, but are not limited to:

- **Demons cause oppression** - They can place an overwhelming burden your life which is intended to manipulate and control the way you act, think, feel or function. They put heaviness and hardships on you in order to weigh you down and cause you to give up.

- **Demons inflict suppression** - They can act as a force that comes to resist you and work against you in order to stop your progress or keep you from advancing in life.

- **Demons bring afflictions** - They can cause prolonged hurt, pain, suffering, grief, illness or failing heath and misery. They can also sabotage your life and cause the loss of loved ones, marriages, businesses and jobs which adds sorrows.

Whenever a demon comes to attack your life, its ultimate plan is to cause discomfort, discouragement or even death.

Therefore whenever they come there are several things that they will attempt to do:
- Demons cause sadness.
- Demons can cause unbearable misery and anguish.
- Demons incite fear and inflict torment.
- Demons cause stress and anxiety.
- Demons can cause you to rehearse negative experiences; they do not want you to recover from stressful situations or tragedies.
- Demons inflict pain and agony.

- Demons defile; they produce filthy thoughts in the realm of the mind and imagination driving people to think evil, nasty thoughts about others and even negative, nasty thoughts about themselves.
- Demons cause hardships.
- Demons ensnare your life.
- Demons bind and cause bondage.
- Demons entice or temp you to do evil.
- Demons harass you.
- Demons deceive you; they provoke pride and instigate guilt or shame.
- Demons weaken you; they cause lethargy and weariness in the soul.
- Demons cause sleepiness especially when it is time to pray or study your bible.
- Demons cause weariness of the mind, mind battles and discouragement.
- Demons cause gross weariness, fatigue and "prayerlessness"; they create distractions when it is time to pray or read your Bible.
- Demons drive and compel you to engage in excessive uncontrolled habits known as compulsive disorders. There are many

negative habits such as: compulsive eating, (over eating-gluttony, under eating-anorexia) eating dirt, feces, paper, flour; lying, talking, smoking, drinking and more.

• Demons compel, persuade, influence, suggest, twist, pervert the truth, and so much more.

DEMONIC INFILTRATION
Three Arenas In Which Demons Can Infiltrate And Torment You

   A. **Mental Torment**-Causes fear, mental anguish and confusion in the mind.
   B. **Physical Torment**-Causes severe sickness, chronic illness, and excruciating pain in the body.
   C. **Spiritual Torment**-Causes, guilt and condemnation; fear of failing God.

Demons enslave you and cause you as a Christian to live a lifestyle of iniquity where you keep falling in and out of sin, such as:

fornication, masturbation, lying and more. Their main purpose is to seek to afflict you and bring your life into hardship or bondage.

There are several classifications of demons, some of which may include but are not limited to:

- **Deaf and Dumb spirits** seek to *limit* your progress and advancement; the strongman in operation is the spirit of fear

- **Unclean spirits** *bind* and limit your mobility; these are spirits which prevent and twist the mind.

- **Tormenting spirits** seek to *attack* your mind, bringing you under their demonic control

- **Evil spirits** will totally *overtake* and possess you, causing you to become heartless as you perform heinous crimes, violent acts and sexual behaviors. These spirits will also *drive* you to the point where you become compulsive and obsessive in your behavior

- **Seducing spirits** will go to any extent to discourage you in an effort to *lure, drag* or *entice* you to abandon your kingdom assignment and, eventually to cause you to move away from the Kingdom of God

- **Sabotaging spirits** – these spirits are sent to your life for the purpose of destroying you. Sabotage is the deliberate destruction of or action taken to undermine, hinder or destroy something or somebody's efforts and achievements

- **Lucific angels** – these are evil spirits that are a part of Lucifer's demonic kingdom and work on his behalf to carry out his commands

- **Familial spirits** - these spirits travel in and down the family from bloodline from generation to generation and can actively operate in your life by manifesting diseases, hardships, misfortunes and other negative experiences which may drastically limit you. If there are negative "traits" you can identify which manifest in different members of the same family this is, more than likely, a familial spirit. For example, there may be an ailment or unusual traits which are common to all members of a family, such as cancer, diabetes, high blood pressure and the like. Likewise, there may be patterns of extreme poverty and other maladies which loom over a family from generation to generation. These oppressive traits can remain common among family members no matter how talented, gifted or educated they are or how they seek to break free from it. Many people make the gross mistake of taking ownership of these demonic spirits by making statements such as, *"That's just the way I am"* or *"Everybody in my family struggles with this"* or *"All the men in my family die young"*, not knowing that they are inviting unclean or familial spirits to their lives

- **A Familiar spirit** - this is a spirit that is sent by wicked powers; either the devil, himself, witches or other occult workers to attack you, your family, business or ministry. Further, familiar spirits can act as informants to witches and other occult workers who are tapping into the realm of darkness in order to gain information about you. These can be monitoring spirits who seek out ways to afflict, harm or oppress you. They are sent to wreak havoc in your life in an effort to totally destroy. In turn, this *spirit* which is a divining demon, after being conjured up, gives this information to a sorcerer, witch or spirit guide

■ **Spiritism, Spiritualists and Demonic Spirits** – Ungodly spiritual practices, such as necromancy, clairvoyance and psychic revelation were believed to come to certain *"gifted"* members of a family. However, what many do not realize is that these powers or abilities originate from the satanic kingdom of darkness and were given to them by a demon or *familiar spirit* that satan has assigned to destroy their family line *(Leviticus 20:27; 1 Samuel 28:8)*

HOW DO DEMONS ENTER

As believers we are engaged in spiritual warfare on a daily basis. The war between the kingdom of darkness and the kingdom of light is for ultimate possession of your soul. Demonic spirits from the realm of darkness seek to enter your life in order to cause harm.

As a believer, demons can only enter your life if you open yourself to an attack and give it legal rights to enter. This simply means that you can do things to cause demons to enter your life. The Bible warns in *Ecclesiastes 10:8* that if you break the hedge, the serpent will bite you.

In other cases, ungodly circumstances outside of what you do can leave your life vulnerable to demonic infiltration. Some things that can cause demonic access to your life include, but are not limited to the following:

DEMONS ENTER THROGH OPEN DOORWAYS AND GATEWAYS TO THE SOUL

He that hath no rule over his own spirit is like a city that is broken down, and without walls. (Proverbs 25:28)

1. **Disobeying God's Word** which includes partial obedience as well as delayed obedience
2. **Practicing willful sin** or iniquity, such as fornication, adultery, lewd lust, sexual activities *(this also includes: pornography, masturbation, homosexuality, lesbianism, bestiality, effeminate behavior in males, perversion, inordinate affections-which are passions and desires that are not ordained by God)*
3. **Consulting with Occult Workers:** such as witches, psychics, mediums, soothsayers, palm readers, tea leave readers, spiritualists
4. **Dishonoring Your Parents:** *(this includes both your biological and spiritual parents or spiritual leadership)*

5. **Communicating Perversely** - the words we speak can activate godly or demonic activity in our lives or in the life of someone else. There are several demonic characteristics which can be tied to the tongue, some of which includes: profanity, a lying spirit (pathological liars-people who lie about everything); gossiping spirit, blasphemy, exaggeration, and more

6. **Engaging In Occult Practices**, including: reading horoscopes, gambling, pledging to secret societies, such as lodges, fraternities, sororities and other covert organizations

7. **Succumbing to Curses** rendered by witches or other evil people

8. **Inheriting Generational or Ancestral Curses**; also known as bloodline or foundational curses. These curses are passed down the generational blood line through the womb

9. **Pronouncing self-inflicted curses** these occur when you speak against your own self

10. **Experiencing pre-natal influences** from evil spirits attacking the womb; resentment or rejection from the womb; mother experiencing pregnancy trauma or shock; unexpected fearful events, abuse, major disappointment during pregnancy

11. **Experiencing childhood abuse** of any kind, including verbal, physical, mental, emotional or sexual abuse

12. **Enduring negative soulish powers** where parents are possessive, manipulative and controlling

13. **Suffering in your emotions -** Demons seek to negatively affect your emotions in order to demobilize your life. When your emotions come under the control of evil spirits, you will begin exhibiting spirits of anger, fear, loneliness, jealousy, low self-esteem and more. You may also exhibit spirits of bitterness, rejection (including, despair, hurt, suicide, etc.); rebellion (including, hatred, anger, violence, pride, offense, etc.); resentment (holding grudges, spitefulness, etc.)

14. **Through the arena of the mind** – demonic spirits can attack your mind through ungodly or erroneous thoughts. These thoughts can become demonic strongholds which cause the individual to become resistant to change or even hearing the "truth" of God. The mind is a battlefield. It is there where demons war against the truth and divine will and purpose of God for your life. Relentless demonic spirits release unbelief, doubt, confusion, insanity, discouragement, depression and more. The Word of God reveals in *2 Corinthians 10:4–6* that we are to "cast down imaginations or images and every "high thing" that exalts itself against the knowledge of God and bring into captivity **every thought** to the obedience of Christ. Mental images, imaginations and thoughts are all housed in the "high place" of the mind

15. **Through the dream realm** - demonic spirits can also enter your soul through your dreams. Your dreams are open windows, corridors and doorways to your

soul and ultimately your life. Your dreams represent activity in the subconscious and spiritual realms. Dreams can act as prophetic pointers to show you the will of God for your life and likewise your dreams can become an open portal through which the enemy can infiltrate your life. In *Matthew 13:25*, the Bible reveals that **"while men slept"** the enemy sowed demonic seeds. These seeds, images or symbols may have appeared in your dream but can manifest undue stress, worry, frustration or confusion in the natural if you do not steadfastly resist them; driving the enemy and his demonic plans out of your life. Until you have gone through complete and total deliverance do not be led by your dreams. If you are not delivered, demons, most times use the dream realm to ensnare or entrap you

16. **Through OPEN GATEWAYS CALLED SENSORY RECEPTORS.** These receptors capture information that will influence you to walk in the ways of God's kingdom of

light or, on the other hand, the ways of satan's kingdom of darkness. *Your natural sensory receptors include but are not limited to:*

* ❖ *Through the eyes* – spirits can enter a person through what they see; for example through tragic experiences, traumatic events or experiences, perverted movies, etc.

* ❖ *Through the ears* – spirits can enter a person through what they hear; for example listening to profanity, verbal abuse, negative words spoken against you, and may also include sexually explicit communications, etc.

* ❖ *Through the pores (skin)* – spirits can enter a person through touch. Some people had demonic lotions, potions or powders rubbed on them to either attract favor or the affection of the opposite sex and more

* ❖ *Through the mouth* – spirits can enter a person through what they eat or drink. Sometimes persons may have unknowingly eaten or drank something

that was *"fixed"* with witchcraft poison in order to cause harm to the body and, which cannot be traced or detected by medical investigation, science or technology

DEMONS CAN ENTER IN GANGS

Demons can also operate as organized gangsters. They operate like terrorists cells. In other words, when you find one, keep digging, I guarantee you will discover an entire band or cluster of them. They are organized and have a strongman or commander-in-chief with a battalion and host of other evil spirits with them.

They seldom break their ranks. In other words, these demonic spirits take their assignment serious and will spend decades perfecting their diabolical skills until the appointed time given to them to destroy you. They form what I call "demonic sleeper cells" and operate in stealth mode just like terrorist groups. They enter your city, schools or family and will lie dormant   until they are ready to launch an attack and take over.

TIME-RELEASED CURSES

The sleeper cells are the band of demons who wait for a specific time to unleash their terror in your life. They release time sensitive curses that erupt in an individual's life causing a demonic manifestation on a designated day and time.   Everyone is in shock and surprise because no one saw it coming.

The person hosting these time-released curse may begin to act out in ungodly ways. Others may experience a serious tragedy or trauma which adversely affects their life and the lives of everyone around them. It then becomes a painful dilemma at an unexpected or inconvenient time and season of your life.

You can reverse every curse from over your life by standing in faith and praying a powerful prayer of deliverance.

DEMONOLOGY & DREAMS

"Demonology" is simply the study of demons, their characteristics and how they seek to operate in the life of an individual to bring that person's life into bondage.

A dream is a symbol that something has happened in the realm of the spirit that is about to manifest in your life.

In this subconscious realm, when you are in a somewhat vulnerable state, the enemy seeks every opportunity to launch a demonic attack against your life through the dream realm. As a result, you may have nightmares, torments or other forms of attacks in your dreams.

HOW DEMONS MANIPULATE YOUR DREAMS

Here are some things which may manifest in your dream to indicate that you are under a demonic attack:

- You may dream that you are married to someone other than your spouse
- You may dream that you are falling from a high place and cannot stop yourself from falling
- You may dream that you are in a dungeon or pit and cannot get out
- You may dream that you see people who you know are dead, or who have died a long time ago
- You may dream that you are given food to eat or after eating something in your dream and waking up, you may feel like what you ate was harmful
- You may dream that you are talking to, eating with or negotiating with the dead.
- You may dream that someone cut your clothes or stole something from you.

HOW DEMONS MANIPULATE YOUR DREAMS cont'd...

- You may dream that someone cut your hair and when you wake up you find your head or hair cut.
- You may wake up and continually feel like you have had sex.
- You may find yourself carrying heavy loads of luggage or baggage
- You may find yourself amongst animals in your dream.
- You find yourself frantically swimming in water, sometimes dirty water or you may feel like you are drowning in water in your dream.
- In your dream, someone or something is chasing you or you are running.
- You may dream that you are wearing a mask or involved in a masquerade.
- You dream that you are constantly and intensely fighting.
- You may dream you have been shot in your dream.

HOW DEMONS MANIPULATE
YOUR DREAMS cont'd...

* You may dream that you are being stabbed in your dream.
* You may dream that you are in an accident.
* You dream that you are in a coffin, that you are dead or that you are around dead people.
* You dream that you have been running for long distances or for an extended period of time.
* You dream that your body parts are falling off. (For example, your teeth are falling out.)
* You dream you are counting money in the dream but you do not own the money.
* You dream you are constantly failing.
* You dream you are in the bed of affliction or that you are in the hospital.
* You may dream that you are being suffocated and you cannot breathe.

HOW DEMONS MANIPULATE YOUR DREAMS cont'd...

- You dream you are in a car, a train, or a plane going nowhere or you end up nowhere.
- You dream you are constantly in a dry place, like a wilderness or desert.

If any of the above-mentioned images appear in your dream, this may be an indication that the enemy is seeking to infiltrate your life with some type of oppression, hardship or affliction.

Recurring demonic symbolisms in your dreams can also indicate that your ancestors may have engaged in ungodly or occult practices which have spiritually contaminated your lineage.

For example, your demonic dreams could be coming because your family was involved in witchcraft practices or the occult. This ungodly contamination leaves you vulnerable to the attacks of the enemy, not only in your dreams but, ultimately, in your life. It may, therefore, be necessary to "clean up" and purge your dream realm or dream portal through prayer and fasting.

In other instances, due to the extent of the spiritual offense, you should seek deliverance from a greater spiritual authority such as your pastor or God's Apostles and Prophets who are anointed to deliver you and break generational curses from over your life and the life of your family.

SPIRITUAL GENETIC RE-MODIFICATION OF THE SOUL
(See more in upcoming book by author, "Deliver Us From All Evil")

Several years ago the spirit of the Lord spoke to me about how demons enter the life of a person and alter their entire molecular structure; adversely affecting their progress and ultimate destiny in God. Recently, during a mind-blowing deliverance session, a young lady stood before me who at the time was merely skin and bones. She had lost over thirty pounds and was currently weighing less than one hundred pounds. This woman was noticeably disfigured and could barely stand up.

As I began to deliver her in Jesus' name, an angry demon manifested and shouted, *"We live in this body and have taken her beautiful face and turned it backwards into something that is ugly and unattractive."*

To everyone's surprise the evil spirits confessed that for over a period of several years, that they, through a wicked witchcraft altar, using a human sacrifice, were able to alter this woman's entire life. She was no longer able to digest hard food but was only able to consume puree's and juices made in a blender.

After she received deliverance, we gave her solid food to eat immediately during her deliverance session. Not only was she able to eat the solid food, her body was also able to digest it...*To God Be All The Glory!*

CHAPTER THREE

WHAT IS AN ALTAR?

An *altar* is a consecrated, sacred place where dedicated sacrifice and gifts are offered upon to a god or deity. Altar in Hebrew is **mizbeah** (pronounced miz-bay-akh) and means an altar or to slay. In the Greek, altar is **thusiasterian** meaning an altar as a place of sacrifice.

A *sacrifice* represents an act of slaughtering an animal or person; a place to offer or surrender a possession as an offering to a deity in exchange for a benefit, such as blessings, protection, prosperity, favor and the like.

Throughout scripture, God always required a holy sacrifice from the Children of Israel. That sacrifice often involved an animal of sort; whether a bullock, dove, goats, etc. The shedding of blood represented some living thing was willing to pay a price so that others could be forgiven and freely live.

And almost all things are by the law purged
with blood; and without shedding of blood is
no remission. (Hebrews 9:22)

However, when Jesus shed His blood and gave His life on the Cross, He became the ultimate sacrifice. Therefore, God no longer required animal sacrifices in order for sins to be remitted. Instead, He wants you and I to present our bodies as a living sacrifice in dedication to Him; this is now the sacrifice that God requires of us.

Altars for godly worship or the ungodly practice of worshipping idols was common throughout the Bible. In *2 Kings 23:12* the young king Josiah breaks down the false altars of idolatry or where demonic activities were practiced and erected godly altars. In *Acts 17:23*, the Apostle Paul found many altars erected on Mars Hill in Ephesus; including altars to the unknown God.

In *Exodus 30:1–10*, the altar of incense was erected and offerings were made on behalf of the children of Israel unto Jehovah,

God. The burning incense represented the prayers of the saints. Consistent, fervent prayer attracts the presence of God and brings deliverance. *(Psalm 141:2, Revelation 5:8, Revelation 8:3-4)*

In *Leviticus 6:9*, Aaron, the priest was commanded to never let the fire on the altar burn out. It was to remain lit all through the night until the morning.

DEMONIC ALTARS AND FOUNDATIONS VS HOLY ALTARS

I believe that whatever altar is erected in your honor is what controls everything that is happening in your life. There are either demonic altars erected against you which are bringing you into bondage or holy, godly altars which bring you into deliverance, blessing, breakthrough and prosperity.

- **DEMONIC ALTARS** - Demonic altars are set apart places built by wicked people for the specific intent and purpose of engaging in occult or dark practices. For the most part they are controlled by witches and warlocks, who, for their own gain seek to bring pain and harm upon the life of others. Demonic altars upon which sacrifices have been made can cause sickness, pain, separation, hardship, failure, defeat in the life of an individual and his family

• **HOLY ALTARS -** Holy Altars are built by godly men and women in honor of God and His Son, Jesus, the Christ in order to bring Him glory. God honors holy altars upon which sacrifices and prayers are made to Him. Dedicated holy altars of prayer can cause great deliverance to take place. These holy altars will bring blessings, favor, wealth, increase, prosperity, health, healing and more. Further, these altars are erected in order to offer up worship to God and to seek His presence; to counter the attacks of the enemy and to attract the presence of God to your life.

- **FAMILY/ANCESTRAL ALTARS & FOUNDATIONS -** Family altars are erected by the ancestors on behalf of their family. These can either be holy altars, activated by prayer and sacrifices to God or these can be demonic altars activated by animal or human sacrifices offered to idols. The family foundation can also determine the outcome of many generations. If the family's origin was evil and built on ungodly practices, this will attract demonic bondages to several members of the family throughout its generations until these demonic altars are destroyed. Similarly, if demonic pacts, covenants and altars were erected by a family's ancestors, this will also open the door to evil propensities and demonic activity throughout a family's generations.

For example, some families may have gifted members but they are all in poverty. In other families, the women may be prone to having miscarriages or are barren; for others several members may be bound by debilitating addictions. If demonic family altars and foundations exist in a person's life, they will only be delivered once they stand before a deliverance prophet or spiritual leader who operates from holy, godly altars of prayer, fasting and worship before God.

Many times during deliverance, you will hear me either break or destroy family altars or the altars of witches in order to bring a person or family into deliverance. I am grateful and humbled that God has been anointed and favored me to do so because He taught me how to erect a holy altar in my own life, through prayer and living a consecrated life unto Him.

EVERY KINGDOM IS GOVERNED BY AN ALTAR

Every earthly kingdom is governed or established on the premise of either a wicked altar or a holy altar. Every king has an altar. The decrees, dictates and ordinances of that kingdom are also run by this altar. During bible days, the kings or ruling authorities of that day followed the spiritual counsel of the prophets of God or they ascribed to the counsel of witches, stargazers, false prophets and the like.

The bible has record of many king who did that which was evil or detestable in the sight of God. However, the Word of God further goes on to state that, as King of Israel, Ahab was one of the most wicked kings who had ever ruled. After marrying Jezebel, a high priestess of Baal, Ahab led the nation of Israel into idolatry and pagan worship. Therefore, it is believed that Ahab governed the nation of Israel from a wicked altar. *(1 Kings 16:30)*

BEWARE OF THE SPIRIT OF HEROD

The Herodian Kingdom was established from 37 BC under the leadership of Herod, the Great. Throughout the rulership of the Herodian Kingdom, there were several successors to Herod, the Great including Herod Antipas, Herod Agrippa and others. The Herodian Kings ruled in Judea under the overlordship of the Roman Empire to whom they were socially, economically, militarily and politically subordinate. It was the great Roman Empire that appointed Herod, the Great as King of the Jews.

The culture of the Herodian Kingdom culture was steeped in idolatry, sorcery, and human sacrifice.   Therefore, it was not uncommon for them to engage in animal or human sacrifice. It was Herod Agrippa who martyred James and, because he saw that it pleased the people, also sought to martyr the Apostle Peter.

It was Herod Antipas who had divorced his first wife and taken Herodias, his brother's wife as his own. During Herod's birthday celebration, Salome, the daughter of Herodias, had danced before him and his invited guests. No doubt the dance was not only very seductive but was also a ceremonial gesture steeped in the worship of idols.

Herod was so captivated by the dance ritual that he promised Salome anything she wanted, even up to half his kingdom. Consulting with Herodias, her mother, on what she should request, her mother told her to ask for the head of John, the Baptist.

22 And when the daughter of the said Herodias came in, and danced, and pleased Herod and them that sat with him, the king said unto the damsel, Ask of me whatsoever thou wilt, and I will give it thee.

23 And he sware unto her, Whatsoever thou shalt ask of me, I will give it thee, unto the half of my kingdom.

*24 And she went forth, and said unto her
mother, What shall I ask? And she said, The
head of John the Baptist.*

*25 And she came in straightway with haste
unto the king, and asked, saying, I will that
thou give me by and by in a charger the head
of John the Baptist. (Mark 6:22-25)*

It was John, the Baptist who had stood for righteousness and spoken out against Herodias' marriage to her brother-in-law, Herod Antipas, the then ruling king. As a result of her desire for bitter revenge against the man of God, she told Salome to ask for his head on a platter.

This cruel request for the beheading of John, the Baptist was an ungodly act and, again, indicative of the demonic ruling principalities of that day seeking to destroy the leadership of the early church and the one who would set them free. This also revealed that Herod was an enemy of God and ruled from a demonic altar that sought to destroy the Kingdom of God and God's servants in the earth.

And from the days of John the Baptist until now the kingdom of heaven suffereth violence, and the violent take it by force.
(Matthew 11:12)

The spirit of the Herods that relentlessly seeks to destroy the Kingdom of God, still lives on today. Although, the evil Herodian Kingdom is no longer ruling, the spirit of the Herods continue to wage a bitter war against the advancement of the people of God.

MESSIAH IS HERE
"... and Has Come To Deliver You!"

For decades the Jews had waited and looked for their Messiah and Deliverer to come. The Prophet Isaiah had prophesied that The Messiah would establish His earthly kingdom and rule as a Wonderful Counselor, a Mighty God, the Everlasting Father and the Prince of Peace.

6 For unto us a child is born, unto us a son is given: and the government shall be upon his shoulder: and his name shall be called Wonderful, Counsellor, The mighty God, The everlasting Father, The Prince of Peace.

7 Of the increase of his government and peace there shall be no end, upon the throne of David, and upon his kingdom, to order it, and to establish it with judgment and with justice from henceforth even for ever.
(Isaiah 9:6-7)

Jesus, the Christ is *Yeshua Hamashiach*, the Anointed One with the anointing, or better, the One who brings the anointing with Him to anoint mortal beings. He came to bring deliverance, which He refers to as *Children's Bread or the Children's blessing,* first to the Jews and then to the Gentiles. The Ministry of Jesus, the Christ is the Ministry of Deliverance.

The One who was anointed and sent by God to save His people. He would be called King of the Jews and was sent with a divine mandat to set His people free. This was extremely intimidating to Herod because, as revealed in the prophecy, the kingdom of this Messiah would never end. This is why King Herod wanted to kill Jesus.

Herod represented a demonic ruling principality assigned over that region to fight against the power and authority of the Anointed One; in an effort to block the deliverance of the Jews.

Like every evil order, Herod built a demonic altar in the realm of the spirit by issuing a decree to kill every male child. This included a ritualistic practice of human sacrifice steeped in idolatry and witchcraft.

This wicked decree originating from a demonic altar also demonstrated the human sacrifices that Herod was willing to offer in exchange for the security of his throne and subsequent rulership.

Today, the spirit of Herod continues to fight against the Ministry of Deliverance and it continues to fight against you, as a believer in an effort to sabotage your deliverance and, ultimately, your life. Your enemy does not want to see you set free so he will continue to fight to keep you in bondage. However, the Word of God ensures us that Jesus Christ has come to destroy every work of the devil.

> *For this purpose the Son of God was manifested, that he might destroy the works of the devil. (1 John 3:8)*

CHAPTER FOUR

I AM A CHRISTIAN...WHY DO I NEED DELIVERANCE?

During my time of ministry, I have encountered many believers who have asked if Christians can have demons or if Christians even need deliverance?

When you accept Jesus Christ as Lord and personal Savior, you are saved and have an eternal home with God. In *Romans 10:9, 10*, the Bible reveals that if we confess the Lord Jesus with our mouth and believe in our hearts that God has raised Jesus from the dead that we are saved. This is God's ultimate plan of salvation.

However, while you are here on earth, you will experience some level of attack, oppression or bondage from the enemy that you will need to be set free from. In the truest sense of the meaning of Christian you, as a believer, may not be totally possessed by a demon but you can be, what I refer to as, demonized.

When you become demonized you are not in a spiritual state where you are totally unaware that you have been overtaken or controlled by a demonic spirit. However, when you are demonized you are in a spiritual condition where you become afflicted, affected or influenced by demonic spirits.

These evil spirits try to afflict your life and the lives of your family and loved ones to bring hurt, pain, rejection, depression, anxiety, disappointment, discouragement, stress, generational curses, sicknesses, infirmity, diseases, disorders, witchcraft oppression, poverty and lack, depression, fear, anxiety, addiction, anger, rage and the like.

> *For this purpose the Son of God was manifested, that he might destroy the works of the devil.*
> *(1 John 3:8b)*

Therefore, the Spirit of God comes to supernaturally deliver you and set you free from every bondage that the enemy seeks to place upon your life as a believer, and to give you the abundant life that God has promised to you in **John 10:10.**

> *[10] The thief cometh not, but for to steal, and to kill, and to destroy: I am come that they might have life, and that they might have it more abundantly.*

EXPOSING THE SPIRIT OF WITCHCRAFT

We are living in a time when it seems as though people are becoming more evil. In previous years, whenever family members, neighbors or coworkers had a disagreement, all parties involved may have engaged in a heated argument or even become a little physical. However, today many people seem to be dealing with disagreements by afflicting the other person with witchcraft.

Little regard is shown for the principles of the Kingdom of God and many people are giving themselves over to dark counsel in order to resolve issues, get answers or seek out revenge. What many fail to understand is that when they engage the demonic realm they are attracting demonic spirits to their lives and opening the door for various types of maladies to afflict, not only their lives, but their entire lineage.

These unfortunate events may manifest in the form of unexpected accidents, sudden traumas, tragedies, misfortunes or even death.

Time and time again, God warned the children of Israel not to engage in any dark practices, including witchcraft and the occult.

> *9When thou art come into the land which the LORD thy God giveth thee, thou shalt not learn to do after the abominations of those nations.*

> *10There shall not be found among you any one that maketh his son or his daughter to pass through the fire, or that useth divination, or an observer of times, or an enchanter, or a witch.*

> *11Or a charmer, or a consulter with familiar spirits, or a wizard, or a necromancer.*

12For all that do these things are an abomination unto the LORD: and because of these abominations the LORD thy God doth drive them out from before thee.
(Deuteronomy 18:9-12)

Every witch has an altar. Witches and other wicked people all erect altars upon which they consult and offer sacrifices. These sacrifices are offered in order to manipulate and control your life. Whenever an altar is consulted, a covenant, pact or agreement is forged.

The Spirit of God strongly warns that practicing any form of witchcraft is an abomination. Many people are under mental and emotional bondages because they are bound by demonic spirits and witchcraft attacks.

People, for the most part, who are affected by this practice do not want to be bound and are crying to be set free.

*If my people, which are called by my name,
shall humble themselves, and pray, and seek
my face, and turn from their wicked ways;
then will I hear from heaven, and will forgive
their sin, and will heal their land.*
(2 Chronicles 7:14)

If we are going to be able to gain the victory in our lives we are going to have to rise up in spiritual authority and begin to pray. I firmly believe that *"prayer not only changes things, but fervent prayer can change everything!"*

HOW TO KNOW WHEN YOU ARE UNDER A WITCHCRAFT ATTACK

*"Witchcraft is the use of various kinds of supernatural or magical powers in order to **manipulate, dominate, intimidate or control** someone else's life.* Further, "witchcraft" is the use of devices such as words, religion or culture to force someone to function outside of their will. It causes oppression, and can ultimately lead to destruction.

- **Manipulation** – means to be under the stronghold of someone or something that is forcing you to act or respond outside of your own will or desire. In some instances people who perceive themselves as weaker than other persons may tend to use manipulation in order to get what they want because they believe they are unable to attain it directly. The cruel idea of manipulation brings to mind the image of a puppet on a string.

- **Intimidation** – the use of one's power, authority, title, stature or insignia to make someone else feel inferior, fearful or insignificant. It may be the use of words, posture, or position to cause others to feel "less than" or "powerless" to the degree where they are not able to function or cannot fulfill their divine assignment. Intimidators tend to "prey" on the weak in order to keep them under their control and domination.

- **Domination** – to consume the mind, emotions or attention of another by exerting one's power or abilities. It is the illegal, adverse use of one's influence to control or overpower the will of another person.

- **Control** – this occurs when one person blatantly seeks to undermine or override the will and desires of that person to coerce them to perform or carry out an act for their own selfish gain. This type of control is both diabolical and devious. For the most part, a person knows that if he is able to control your mind he will, eventually, control you and ultimately, your destiny.

- **Deception** – this occurs when someone gives you a false sense of hope in something that seems to be good but it is inherently evil. Information is intentionally miscommunicated in order to create an understanding that does not represent the truth

There are various forms of witchcraft which may include Occult Practices, which include hidden or dark practices. If you or a loved one is practicing or has consulted with someone who is involved in witchcraft, once you repent of this sin, the Spirit of God will set you free from this destructive device of the enemy.

In this hour, if you, as a believer do not have an altar erected unto God, upon which prayer if offered, you will succumb to the evil altars of your enemy.

WHAT IS A CURSE?

A curse is said to be a solemn or serious intentional utterance that is intended to invoke affliction or harm on someone. Further, it is an evil spoken word intended to inflict pain, hardship or, even death on the life of a person.

A curse is normally an evil spoken word released with force, authoritative power, a strong conviction or passion. Generational curses come to your life as a result of the sins of your ancestors. These are sins your ancestors committed based on who or what they worshipped, or it is also based on what they believed and practiced.

For example, if they believed in the evil practice of witchcraft and demonic powers; many of them engaged in lewd lustful practice, such as orgies. These practices have opened the doors to the demonic realm in your life and family. Those demons which enter your life through the bloodline are tied to your family altar. A bloodline curse is a method and way in which a curse travels through a family's lineage.

This is why I deal with the foundation and break every family altar. Whatever your family bowed down to, even if it was a hundred years ago, will affect your life now and in the years to come.

The enemy can release a curse over your life in the form of ill-wishes, incantations or negative spoken words. He "hires" people who practice what we call hexcrafts, jinxcrafts, spellcrafts and witchcraft in order to bring harm, misfortune or distress on the life of others. Demonic spirits are accustomed to carrying out these diabolical ill-wishes which cause pain and distress in people's lives. The operate under the instruction or the command of the strongman demon that rules over them.

A curse is the opposite of a blessing *(good fortune, success or wellness)*, it is a prayer or an appeal for evil against your family, business, ministry or life. Just as God uses His true prophets to speak words of blessings, the enemy uses other people, "false prophets" or witches operating in spirits of hatred, jealousy, envy and greed to speak demonic curses over your life.

Every spoken word carries a degree of power, be it negative or positive, and someone's words can either cause you pain or bring you joy. *(Proverbs 18:21)*

How do you know when your life is being affected by a curse?

If you find yourself under an attack by the enemy, in a perpetual struggle or constantly "losing in life" then you should seek to determine if this hardship is the result of a curse that has been released against you.

Whenever something is beyond what may be deemed as a normal or rational conclusion to an adverse experience in your life, then this could be the manifestation of a curse.

For example, if you are experiencing prolonged sickness and your doctors are confused about what is happening to you, then this sickness may be the result of a curse. Furthermore, repeated struggles or failures that depict never-ending cycles of hardship should be investigated.

Some curses are just the work of demons that are searching for a habitation or dwelling place. You must determine their "doors of access" or "avenues of entry" and expel them immediately. Failure to recognize or acknowledge the presence of a curse in your life can lead to your ultimate demise or detriment.

> *"My people are destroyed for lack of knowledge: ..." (Hosea 4:6)*

In, **Hosea 4:6,** the Word of God bears witness that if you are unaware of what is fighting against you, then you may be subject to defeat.

Therefore, if you are going to embrace your generational blessings, you must:

- Expose, acknowledge, confess and Break the curses that had your forefathers bound

- Remember every promise that God spoke to your forefathers

- Become desperate to fight for the blessings of your forefathers

- Seek God for wisdom to acquire the promise (through fasting and prayer)

- Know what your forefathers were entitled to; aggressively pursue it

- Do what is necessary to activate your blessings. (For example, in *Genesis 26:12* the Word of God states that Isaac sowed in the time of famine over and over again. Although his enemies continually sabotaged his efforts he never stopped until by the grace of God, he became established in that land.

FROM GENERATION TO GENERATION

Every human being was born with the chemical gene called DNA. Within your DNA is physical information that describes not only you but others in your generational lineage.

There are physical traits or genetics which pass down through generations, such as hair, eye color, baldness, excess weight, dwarfism and the like. There are also soulical traits, such as behaviors, mannerisms, habits, attitudes, personalities, likes, dislikes, desires, proclivities, such as addictions and more.

There are spiritual traits passed on from generation to generation. There are family spirits called familial spirits which are passed down from generation to generation, through the bloodline.

BLOODLINE CURSES
For the life of the flesh is in the blood: and I have given it to you upon the altar to make an atonement for your souls: for it is the blood that maketh an atonement for the soul.
(Leviticus 17:11)

Whenever you go to a doctor complaining about any type of ailment, the first thing a good doctor will do is order your blood work. Their objective is to see what is happening in your body by testing your blood.

One drop of blood can determine whether you are positive or negative to a disease or disorder.

"The blood never lies", whatever is in your body will show up in your blood.

Today, we, as our ancestors are all given a choice, whether we will walk in the ways of God or if we will choose to go after the ways of darkness. Unfortunately, some of our ancestors chose not to walk in the ways of God, but rather erected demonic altars and began worshipping idols.

These ungodly rituals they sought to teach to or transfer to future generations, not knowing that instead of advancing and prospering, they, instead suffered severe backlash from the forces tied to these family idols.

Some tapped into the realm of darkness to gain power, wealth, prosperity, property and other benefits; even promising to give their future offspring as an offering. They gained the things that they wanted but lost their relationship with God, open the door for curses to enter their family lineage and paid a price that would continue for generations to come.

As a consequence of turning away from the presence of God, they attracted demonic spirits to their lives which resulted in devastating plagues and disorders passing down through our generational lines, called bloodline curses.

The devastating aspect of these types of curses is that they do not only affect the person who activated them in the family line but can affect generations to come.   This means that these curses can affect your children and your children's children.

Some people experience undue hardship, oppression, tragedy, misfortune, failure and other maladies because of these bloodline curses. These persons who were not involved in their ancestor's practices are now experiencing various demonic attacks through no fault of their own.

Many times during my deliverance services, in order to set an individual free, I am instructed by Holy Spirit to break curses from over the lives of parents, grandparents and other ancestors before I can bring that individual into total deliverance.

In serving God, you will receive blessings, favor and prosperity; but if you choose to follow after the kingdom of darkness you will attract curses and demonic oppression to your life and the lives of your children. You will either receive the blessings of the kingdom of light as you serve God or you will be influenced and controlled by demonic spirits from the kingdom of darkness as you serve the devil.

HOW GENERATIONAL CURSES, FAMILIAL & FAMILIAR SPIRITS WORK

Generational curses are brought on as a result of the sins of our ancestors; forefathers or foremothers, back to the third, fourth or fifteenth generation and beyond.

> *I will visit the curses of your forefathers down to the third and fourth generation. (Exodus 20:5-6)*

A generational curse or habit passes through your lineage and flows through your sinful nature. Generational curses manifest in various ways within the family, such as: everybody drinks, are compulsive gamblers; are addicts, compulsive liars or thieves, females who are barren, and more.

Familial spirits are demonic spirits which climb down through the family line, moving from one generation to another. Familiar spirits are demonic spirits which are sent to monitor, watch or gather information from your life or your family. Familiar spirits can also harass you or wreak havoc in your life.

For example they can harass, torment or inflict pain, sickness, or disease, disorders, dilemmas; they can wreak havoc, hardship and destruction on your life or within your family. Most times they are sent by wicked people, such as witches or warlocks; other times they are deviant demons which have come from the realm of darkness, see an opening door in your life, and enter.

Generational curses are also called bloodline curses because they pass through a family's bloodline. Genetic dispositions such as diseases, illnesses, blindness, and other issues are the manifestation of bloodline curses.

You do not have to live with debilitating curses in your life. No matter how a curse manifests in your life, Jesus shed His blood so that you can be totally set free from the bondage of every generational/ancestral or bloodline curse. If you are a believer, it is time to be set free!

CHAPTER FIVE

DELIVERANCE IS ALWAYS NECESSARY

Everyone at some time in their life will need deliverance. Deliverance is a lifestyle and an essential component of your spiritual journey and existence as you confront the day to day challenges of life. As you attain greater blessings, achieve more in life or seek to go after the things of God; your adversary, the devil will relentlessly seek to trap, derail or even destroy you, your family or that endeavor that you set out to do for God.

You may discover that at different times and seasons in your life you were delivered from something yet, in another season you need deliverance from some other type of demonic influence. For example, as a single woman, you may have needed deliverance from spirits of lust, perversion and the like, Then, after marrying, you find yourself struggling with spirits of adultery and insecurity.

On the other hand, in one season you may have battled spirits of poverty and lack but have now been delivered from them and yet, after God blesses you with wealth, you may now struggle with spirits of anxiety or even greed. No matter how old or young you are, as a human being you will discover that something is constantly fighting against you.

There is an old adage which says, *"For every level, there is a new devil."* In every stage or level of your spiritual journey, you will discover that you need some form of deliverance. This is the case because as long as you are a believer, as long as you are alive, you will encounter an ongoing war between good and evil or light and darkness.

In fact, it is during these fierce day to day spiritual battles that you may experience attacks from the enemy and become afflicted.

Many are the afflictions of the righteous: but the Lord delivers him out of them all.
(Psalm 34:19)

When these afflictions come, if you are not careful, demons will also seek to take an occasion to enter your life. One of the ways to remove them is through the administration of deliverance.

DELIVERANCE DESTROYS AFFLICTION

Deliverance is the key to eradicate affliction and every demonic attack against your life, your family, your health, your finances and more. In other words, when you receive deliverance, affliction has to leave.

In *Luke 10:19*, when Jesus rose from the dead he gave resurrection power to His faithful disciples, His chosen servants. This resurrection power gave them supernatural ability to heal the sick, heal the lame and raise the dead.

I am he that liveth, and was dead; and,
behold, I am alive for evermore, Amen; and
have the keys of hell and of death.
(Revelation 1:18)

Deliverance is administered to you through the ministry of His true Apostles and Prophets by the power of the blood of Jesus and in the name of Jesus.

Till we all come in the unity of the faith, and
of the knowledge of the Son of God, unto a
perfect man, unto the measure of the stature of
the fulness of Christ: (Ephesians 4:13)

Spiritual growth and development produce absolute maturity. Failing to mature as a Christian will leave you vulnerable to the devices of the enemy. In *Ephesians 4:13*, the writer is simply saying that until we grow up spiritually and learn to live a life totally yielded to the leading, guidance and control of the Spirit of God we will always need some level of deliverance.

Absolute spiritual maturity eventually brings us to a glorified realm in God where we are no longer in any level of bondage but are victorious.

As Jesus taught His disciples to pray in *Matthew 6:10,* He told them to pray to the Father that His kingdom would come and His will be done on earth as it is being done in Heaven.

Your entire existence should reflect the beauty, grace and peace of living according to God's divine blueprint for your life. The more you are delivered from the vices of the enemy the greater will be your ability to reflect His glory as you live the life that God designed for you to live.

THE PROCESS OF DELIVERANCE

Although deliverance may happen instantly, by the supernatural power of God, I have discovered that you may have to walk through various levels and processes in order to come into complete or absolute deliverance. These processes can sometimes take place by divine intervention and at other times, your absolute deliverance may occur over a period of time.

For example, just like salvation, we were saved from our sins but are still dying daily to our carnal nature as our spirit man is being renewed day by day.

When Jesus returns we will all be saved from this evil world; this is another level or dimension of salvation. So, yes, once we accept Christ as our Lord and personal Savior, we are saved; this level represents eternal salvation.

As Christians, we are already saved and cannot be saved anymore. However, as we develop and grow in our Christian faith, more carnal or worldly things fall off of us and we become more like Christ as we draw closer to Him. The process of deliverance is the same way.

As demons are cast out of us, we immediately become free of them; but, if for some reason we find ourselves under another attack of other forces of darkness, we do not hold onto or claim them as or own, we seek deliverance from them in Jesus' name.

In other words, even though a demon is cast out of your life and it leaves, your process of wholeness and transformation will involve radical steps, such as:

- repenting from every ungodly practice or sin in your generational line
- renouncing any current involvement in the occult
- forgiving everyone who has ever hurt you, including yourself
- engaging in fervent prayer and fasting
- renewing your mind according to the Word of God
- separating yourself from some people, places or organizations
- removing demonic points of contact such as charms, pendants, clothing, artifacts, and the like

•striving to live a life that attracts the presence of God

DELIVERANCE FROM CURSES, SPELLS AND ANCESTRAL COVENANTS OF FAMILY ALTARS

Deliverance is necessary when you are under a demonic attack or tormented by any unexplainable, repetitive vicious cycle. If your attack originated when your ancestors dedicated you before idols or on a wicked altar, the demonic entities attached to that evil altar comes back to block, hinder and seek to destroy you.

Whenever you are being delivered from ancestral spirits, demonic generational curses, powers of witchcraft, demonic family altars and foundations you must recognize that there may be demonic forces from your family altar which are fighting you. You must be prepared to denounce all ties with your family altar and fully embrace the Spirit of God for your total deliverance

THE PROPHETIC DELIVERER

In every dispensation, God raises up His Apostles and Prophets with the anointing to deliver His people.

> 18 *The Spirit of the Lord is upon me, because he hath anointed me to preach the gospel to the poor; he hath sent me to heal the brokenhearted, to preach deliverance to the captives, and recovering of sight to the blind, to set at liberty them that are bruised,*
>
> 19 *To preach the acceptable year of the Lord.* (Luke 4:18 - 19)

In *Luke 4:18*, Jesus reveals the nature of His earthly mission which is the ministry of deliverance. To the people of His day, He made a public declaration that He had come as their Deliverer, anointed to set the captives free. Later, He would anoint several of His apostles, such as the Apostle Peter and the Apostle Paul, to also preach the gospel and cast out demons.

Today, the Spirit of God continues to anoint His servants, the Apostles and Prophets, to continue the Ministry of Jesus. These Apostles and Prophets are mantled with a unique gift of supernatural power to cast out devils and to set every captive free.

> *16 He that believeth and is baptized shall be saved; but he that believeth not shall be damned.*
>
> *17 And these signs shall follow them that believe; In my name shall they cast out devils; they shall speak with new tongues;*
> *(Mark 16:16 - 17)*

The Spirit of God releases the anointing upon whomever He chooses to operate in this powerful gift of the spirit. You should be very careful when dealing with demonic spirits and entities. The anointing of deliverance and casting out demons is not an automatic spiritual endowment. It is an area of Ministry to which you must be called.

WARNING!!
IMPORTANT DETAILS TO REMEMBER!!

DO NOT ATTEMPT TO CAST OUT DEMONS ESPECIALLY IF YOU HAVE NOT BEEN ANOINTED BY GOD OR TRAINED TO DO SO. IF YOU FEEL YOU NEED DELIVERANCE YOU SHOULD PRAY AND SEEK GOD FOR A TRUE PROPHET WHO IS ANOINTED AND CALLED BY GOD TO MINISTER OR ADMINISTER DELIVERANCE AND CAST OUT DEVILS!!

THE MINISTRY OF DELIVERANCE IS A DIVINE CALLING

Many people seem to be fascinated by the deliverance ministry and casting out demons. I would like to issue a very strong warning that you or no one you know should seek to engage in casting out devils unless you are called by God and have been trained by an Apostle or Prophet to do so.

11 And God wrought special miracles by the hands of Paul:

12 So that from his body were brought unto the sick handkerchiefs or aprons, and the diseases departed from them, and the evil spirits went out of them.

13 Then certain of the vagabond Jews, exorcists, took upon them to call over them which had evil spirits the name of the Lord Jesus, saying, We adjure you by Jesus whom Paul preacheth.

14 And there were seven sons of one Sceva, a Jew, and chief of the priests, which did so.
r
15 And the evil spirit answered and said, Jesus I know, and Paul I know; but who are ye?

16 And the man in whom the evil spirit was leaped on them, and overcame them, and prevailed against them, so that they fled out of that house naked and wounded.
(Acts 19:11-16)

Demonic entities are vicious and will go to any lengths to inflict pain, hardship and even death upon your life. God equips His servants to skillfully dethrone every power of darkness, in Jesus' name.

PRAYER OF DELIVERANCE
HOW TO BREAK AND REVERSE EVERY CURSE FROM YOUR LIFE

You must seek out the assistance of a prophet of God who is anointed and equipped to deliver you. However, you can pray this powerful prayer of deliverance to break and reverse demonic curses from over your life:

- I bind and destroy the powers of the family demon from over my life, in the name of Jesus

- by the blood of Jesus, I destroy the covenant that was made with that demonic spirit

- I renounce, break up and totally destroy the demonic family altar that I was dedicated on by the fire of Holy Ghost

- I destroy the idol and the powers of the idol which are tied to that covenant or altar, by the power of the Holy Ghost.

- I pray to be delivered from the altars of my father's house and my mother's house, in Jesus name.

- I destroy every blood covenant that was made, even on the day I was born.

- I break every demonic pact, credence and agreement that were made by my ancestors which adversely affected my life. I burn their contracts and diabolical plans to block, stop or manipulate my progress, in Jesus name.

- I command every demonic mark they have placed on me or my body to disappear now in Jesus' name

- I break, destroy and cancel every spell or curse from over my life by the power of Holy Spirit in Jesus' name.

- I command every demonic power to release me, my family and my destiny, in Jesus' name.

- I remove my name and the name of each member of my family who has been dedicated on every demonic altar.

- I remove my name from every demonic registry, book or diary.

- I remove the powers of darkness off of my photos, or anything else belonging to me in Jesus' name.

- I pray against ancient spirits, deities and ancestral serpent spirits, in Jesus' name

- I pray against the spirit of the worm and burn it by the fire of Holy Ghost

- I command the wicked powers of every demonic family idol to fall down and die, in Jesus' name

- I command every demonic family altar and foundation to be destroyed by the fire of the Holy Ghost, in Jesus' name.

- I command the serpent to uncoil itself from around my life and the life of my children. In Jesus' name I command it to be totally destroyed by the fire of the Holy Ghost

- I declare every curse in my family lineage to be destroyed in the name of Jesus.

- I declare that the curses of my ancestral lineage be destroyed in my generation, in the name of Jesus.

- I activate the blessings and favor of God in my life and the life of my children down to the fifteenth generation and beyond

- I command my soul, my mind, my emotions, my health, my wealth and my entire life to prosper right now, in the name of Jesus!

- I command the blessings and favor of Almighty God to overshadow me and prosper me and my family, in the mighty name of Jesus Christ!

Stand on the power of the Word of God. According to *Luke 10:19,* Jesus said Behold I give you power over all the powers of the enemy and nothing shall by any means hurt you.

God has given you power over your enemy. If you feel as though you are being overpowered by the enemy then I encourage you to speak with your pastor or an Apostle or Prophet who is anointed by God to administer deliverance and set the captives free.

Although Jesus has give us power over all the powers of the enemy, there are some stubborn and persistent problems, which I call *hard cases*, that you may need to be delivered from by someone who walks in a greater level of spiritual authority.

MAINTAINING YOUR DELIVERANCE

It is very important that you make every effort to maintain your deliverance. For some people, their deliverance may be a one-time occurrence. For others, their deliverance may be a process and fully manifest over a period of time.

No matter how your deliverance comes, just know that once you are declared free from the bondage of the enemy, you are free. Your deliverance comes to:
- Set you free from demonic bondages, shackles and chains
- Remove the influence of the enemy from your life
- Destroy the plans of the enemy for your life
- Bring you closer to God and His divine will for your life
- Attract the presence of God to your life

Maintaining the presence of God in your life keeps the enemy away from you and opens heaven over your life. In order to cultivate a relationship with God, you must:
- Develop a lifestyle of prayer and pray every day
- Study and meditate on the Word of God

- Live a fasted life
- Testify about the goodness of God in your life
- Obey the Word of God
- Obey the instructions of the Prophet or Spiritual Leader who brought you into deliverance

OVERCOMING DEMONIC SYMPTOMS

Once you have been delivered from the vices of the enemy, you must continue to fight for your deliverance. This is necessary because the enemy will continue to send demonic symptoms to you causing you to feel the sicknesses, aches and pains you had before or experience the physical effects from what you were just delivered.

> 43 *When the unclean spirit is gone out of a man, he walketh through dry places, seeking rest, and findeth none.*

> 44 *Then he saith, I will return into my house from whence I came out; and when he is come, he findeth it empty, swept, and garnished.*

*45 Then goeth he, and taketh with himself
seven other spirits more wicked than himself,
and they enter in and dwell there: and the last
state of that man is worse than the first. Even
so shall it be also unto this wicked generation.*
(Matthew 12:43-45)

The enemy does this, seeking to regain entrance to your life; trying to make you feel as though you are still bound. Once you remain committed to praying everyday, and reading, meditating on and obeying the Word of God and once your atmosphere remains saturated with worship, you will have power to overcome the enemy and rebuke every symptom that tries to attack you.

Once you are able to overcome the demonic attacks and symptoms of the enemy, you must now be prepared to aggressively engage in godly practices that will help you maintain your freedom. These are what I call the principles or *pillars of deliverance.*

THE PILLARS OF DELIVERANCE

Pillars represent the secure foundation, premise or principle upon which something is governed or established. In order for you to maintain your freedom, there are several powerful pillars of deliverance, which I have discovered, in which you must be willing to engage, including, but not limited to:

1. Awareness

Before deliverance can take place, there must be an awareness that exposes the truth that something is wrong in your life and deliverance is necessary.

2. Acknowledgement

Once you become aware of what is wrong in your life, you must be willing to acknowledge it. You must be willing to call it by name. If the real problem is *jealousy* then do not "soften" it by calling it less than what it really is, like low self-esteem.

3. Belief

Hebrews 11:6 admonishes that we must not only believe that God exists, but that He wants to deliver and bless us. Once you believe that Jesus can and will deliver you, then you will receive your deliverance. Doubt and unbelief are the greatest enemies to your deliverance. Your belief that God has delivered you will also be necessary if you are going to maintain any level of deliverance.

4. Confession

In *James 5:16*, the Word of God tells us to confess our faults one to another. Further, it has been said that open confession is good for the soul. Once you have acknowledged what is the real problem that you are wrestling with, then you must be prepared to admit it and begin to deal with it.

5. Humility

You must be able to submit your will, emotions and intellect to what the Spirit of God has done, and is seeking to do in you. Further, you maintain your freedom while continually resisting the deliverance process. God knows what it takes to set you free and to help you maintain your freedom. The Word of God reveals that if we are willing to humble ourselves God will exalt or, better, lift us out of every demonic oppression in due time. *(1 Peter 5:6)*

6. Love

In *Romans 8:32,* the Word of God states that since *God spared not his own Son, but delivered him up for us all, how shall he not with him also freely give us all things?*

God loved us so much that He sacrificed His own Son so that we could receive salvation and deliverance. *(John 3:16)* Embracing the love of God will also help you maintain your deliverance. When you perceive that God truly loves you and wants you to be delivered, you will then begin to achieve greater victories in your life.

7. Forgiveness

If there are issues and challenges in your life arising from what someone else has done to you then you must forgive them. If there are things that you have done to bring hardship on yourself then you must forgive yourself.

Forgiveness is releasing others or yourself from the guilt, weight or oppression from any wrongdoing or offense. However, forgiveness does not require that you remain in relationship with the person, activity or group with which the issue arose. When you forgive the person who offended or hurt you. When you forgive, it releases you from the weight of grudges, bitterness, resentment, animosity, and the like, which the enemy seeks to use to keep you in bondage.

8. Faith

Your faith in God is a necessary part of your deliverance process. When you cannot readily that you are victorious, you will have to believe or trust by faith, that you are delivered and set free. As the enemy seeks to send symptoms to your life, by faith you will have to put on spiritual maturity and power to rebuke what you see and continue to declare your victory.

9. Commitment

At times you may grow weary as you endure the "due process" of your deliverance. Sometimes we instantly set free; however, there are times when God will take us through a process to our deliverance. You must be committed to the process until you are totally set free.

10. Rededication

Once you begin walking through your deliverance, repent of any wrongdoing and seek forgiveness. You must begin to rededicate your life and your self to the things of God. Rededicating and re-committing your life to serving God will continue to remove the enemy's bondage from your life.

11. Consecration

This means to be set apart unto God and can also represent a separation from carnal things in order to be used for a specific purpose, either for a short or extended period of time.

12. Sanctification

You must be prepared to be totally removed from anything or anyone that hinders your deliverance. You must have a *"leave and cleave"* mindset and be prepared to leave whatever you are doing and, then, be consecrated unto God.

13. Holiness

Holiness is the mark of every true believer. Holiness is the standard of living a consecrated and sanctified life that is pleasing to a Holy God who demands that you live according to His plans and precepts for your life. As you are set free from the devices of the enemy you will begin to live more and more in the lifestyle that reflects the glory of God over your life.

14. Righteousness

Living in divine alignment with the will of God in your life brings you into righteousness and holiness. The Word of God says that without faith it is impossible to please God. Your faith and belief in the absolute power of God to deliver and set you free causes you to live in right standing with God. As you experience greater levels of deliverance, your faith in God will help to maintain what he has done in your life.

15. Rejuvenation

It is time to be restored. During this part of the deliverance process you must begin to renew your mind through reading the Word of God. You must seek to cultivate the presence of God in your life. If you do not begin to restore your spirit in the things of God, you may begin to lose the value of the word of deliverance that was spoken to your spirit.

16. Saturation

This means to be soaked, absorbed into, steeped in, immersed, drenched, marinated and dripping. Whatever a thing was soaking in becomes a part of that thing; you become a part of it. Soak in His presence, the Word, praise, worship and prayer. Whatever you become saturated in, you become controlled by. In order to maintain your deliverance, you want to be surrounded by the presence of God because wherever the presence of God is, the enemy cannot stay. Make a daily effort to develop a lifestyle that cultivates His presence.

17. Responsibility

You must take full responsibility for maintaining your freedom. After you have received your deliverance, you must be prepared to build yourself up spiritually and cultivate the presence of God in your life. You must be careful where you go, what you watch and what you hear. You may be required to make personal adjustments to your life, such as moving to another place or separating yourself from people who are a detriment to your life. You must have the courage to do what is necessary to remain free.

18. Accountability

If you are not to the place of personal strength, discipline or maturity to do what you have to in order to maintain your deliverance you should prayerfully consider making yourself accountable to someone else. During your process of recovery it is very important who you allow to speak into your life and to whom you give yourself.

19. Meditation

In *Psalm 1*, the Psalmist declares that in the Word of God is his meditation every day and every night. During times of meditation, you can surround yourself with the things of God. Seeking and obeying godly counsel is very important if you are going to continue to walk in what you received during your time of deliverance. Every day you must spend time understanding your situation in the light of how God sees it and how He sees you, and continue to resist the enemy's influence in your life.

20. Desperation

You have to have a resolute mind that you are going to walk your deliverance through to completion no matter how long it takes. And then, after its completion, you must be willing to fight to maintain your deliverance *"by whatever means necessary!"*

21. Impartation

During the impartation process the Spirit of God will continually form Himself in you. The more you spend time in His presence, the more you will become conformed into the image of His Son, Jesus. Eventually, you will begin to realize that you are no longer seeking Him to deliver and set you free, but you are now seeking after more of Him. As you are now seeking after Him, you will receive a greater measure of His Spirit and begin elevating in the things of God.

CHAPTER SIX

ACCESSING THE BLESSINGS OF GOD

²And I will make of thee a great nation, and I will bless thee, and make thy name great; and thou shalt be a blessing;

³And I will bless them that bless thee, and curse them that curseth thee: and in thee shall all the families of the earth be blessed - (Genesis 12:2, 3)

Every believer has been ordained by God to be blessed. In fact, God has already established a decree and a promise to bless you and your children more and more. The blessings that He has promised to you were intended to extend from one generation to another. As a matter of fact there are *generational blessings* which have been divinely spoken over your life before you were even born.

These precious promises are irrevocable and cannot be changed; they all give you something to look forward to with great anticipation.

This promise He made originated in *Genesis 12* where God makes a covenant with Abraham to bless his seed, for generations to come. This covenant to which every believer is an heir still stands, even today

It is the blessings of God that will make you rich and He adds no sorrow, pain, hardship or distress with them *(Proverbs 10:22).* Life is a blessing and a gift from God and He wants His children to make every effort to enjoy it to the fullest. Once God releases a blessing over your life, no one has the power to curse you.

In *Numbers 22-23* God had already blessed the children of Israel and not even He could reverse it. Balaam, who was a prophet of old, attempted to curse the children of God because he was overtaken by a spirit of greed. No matter how many times he tried, he could not curse them. He eventually conceded and confessed that, *"No one can curse that which God has blessed!"*

GOD WANTS YOU TO BE SAVED

In *2 Peter 3:9b,* the Word of God reveals that it is not His will that any should perish but that all come to know Him in a personal way. When sin first entered the world because of Adam's actions, God immediately activated a plan of salvation that would restore his relationship with mankind. The plan of redemption brought mankind back into right standing with Him.

Whenever we commit any type of sin, this separates us from God. It is not His will that anyone should be separated from Him and suffer as a result. He wants to have covenant relationship and intimate fellowship with His people.

> *For God so loved the world, that he gave his only begotten Son, that whosoever believeth in him should not perish, but have everlasting life. (John 3:16)*

God loves you so much that He gave His Only son to pay the price for your sin so that you can live an abundant life, in right standing with Him, now and throughout eternity.

THE ABC's OF SALVATION

- **A**cknowledge that you are a sinner.
- **B**elieve that Jesus shed His blood and died for you.
- **C**onfess that God has raised Jesus from the grave and He is Lord of your life.

PRAYER OF SALVATION

If you are not saved, open your mouth and pray the following prayer aloud:

- *Father God, have mercy upon me this day according to your loving kindness and your tender mercies; blot out my transgressions and my iniquities (**Psalm 51:1**).*
- *Lord Jesus, I repent of every sin in my life. Please forgive me, wash me with your blood from the inside out, and cleanse me from ALL unrighteousness (**1 John 1:9**).*

- *Jesus I confess with my mouth and believe in my heart that You died and rose from the dead that I might be saved* **(Romans 10:9).**
- *Jesus, I accept and declare that you are Lord and Savior over my life. I renounce Satan as lord over my life and take back ALL of the power over my life that I had given to him, in Jesus' name.*
- *Lord Jesus come into my heart today and baptize me with your Holy Spirit and fire so that I may come into the knowledge of who You are.*
- *Form yourself in me, mighty God. I thank You that You are saving me, even as I cry out to You for Your Word says that they that call upon the name of the Lord shall be saved* **(Acts 2:21)**.
- *Father, I thank you that it is by Your grace that I am saved this day* **(Acts 15:11),** *in Jesus' precious and Holy name I pray AMEN*
- **Now that you have prayed this prayer in faith, you are, right now, a child of God.**

DELIVERANCE BY THE LEGAL BLOOD OF JESUS

There are many key factors which you must engage in order to receive and maintain your deliverance. The ultimate key lies within the legal blood of Jesus, the Christ. I say *legal blood* of Jesus Christ because the shedding of the blood of any other animal or human being for the purpose of tapping into the supernatural realm is considered spiritually illegal. This is why demonic blood covenants and pacts attract demons from the spirit realm to your life.

The blood of Jesus gives you spiritual power of attorney because it is the only recognized and respected spiritual authority that allows you to tap into the supernatural realm and access what you need.

As I administer deliverance, when I declare someone free by the power of the blood of Jesus Christ, I am saying that the supernatural power of God has set them free;

there is no question whether you will gain the victory. We can ascribe your victory to no other force or power. There is no question as to who receives the credit and the glory for setting you free; God Gets All of The Glory!

THE BLOOD SPEAKS

5 Who is he that overcometh the world, but he that believeth that Jesus is the Son of God?

6 This is he that came by water and blood, even Jesus Christ; not by water only, but by water and blood. And it is the Spirit that beareth witness, because the Spirit is truth.

7 For there are three that bear record in heaven, the Father, the Word, and the Holy Ghost: and these three are one.

8 And there are three that bear witness in earth, the Spirit, and the water, and the blood: and these three agree in one.
(1 John 5:5-8)

Heaven and earth both testify to the lordship of Jesus, the Christ. When Jesus died and shed His blood, all heaven and earth recognized His ultimate authority over all things because Jesus represented a life that overcame every evil that exists, including death.

Once you accept Jesus as Lord and Savior, then the victory He won over death, hell and the grave gives you the legal right and authority to overcome every demonic situation you will ever face. When we say that we plead or apply the blood of Jesus, we too are acknowledging that His blood has all power to bring deliverance and activate the Spirit of God to work on our behalf.

As a joint heir with Jesus you inherit every spiritual blessing that is passed down through His bloodline. Pleading the blood of Jesus gives you access to all that God has promised for your life and the life of your family.

DELIVERANCE BY THE NAME OF JESUS

During times of deliverance, I always declare someone free in the name of Jesus the

Christ, The Anointed One who came with an anointing to set every captive free. This indicates that deliverance is coming to that person's life because of Jesus, the Messiah.

In order to maintain your freedom from every demonic oppression through the shed blood of Jesus you must continue to declare that you are free because of Jesus. You have spiritual authority to remind every demonic force that you are no longer bound because Jesus has set you free. Everything in heaven and earth must now line up with your declaration of victory as you continue to declare that you are free in the name of Jesus and by the shed blood of Jesus, Christ.

FREE INDEED
"The Power of The Love of God"

If the Son therefore shall make you free, ye shall be free indeed. (John 8:36)

Once the Spirit of God sets you free, you are free indeed. God uses His servants, the true Prophets as His agents in the earth to declare that you are free.

In order to receive your deliverance and to continue to walk in it, it is important that you first accept the love of God for your life. You must know that God loves you and that His ultimate desire is to see you prosper or succeed in life.

In *3 John 1:2* He says, *"Beloved, I wish above all things that thou mayest prosper and be in health, even as thy soul prospereth!"*

God's ultimate plan is that you enjoy every area of your life. It is not the will of God that His people be bound by the spirit of fear or any demonic power. His love is so powerful that once you accept it, it literally dispels every demonic oppression and infiltration of the enemy in your life. His Word declares in, *2 Timothy 1:7* that, *"God has not given us a spirit of fear but of power, love and a sound mind."*

Once you begin to embrace the love of God you will begin to see greater levels of deliverance manifest in your life. The Spirit of God will begin to flow out of your life and you will walk in *"... love, joy, peace, longsuffering, gentleness, goodness, faith, meekness and temperance: against such there is no law." (Galatians 5:22-23)*

The more you embrace the Spirit of God the less likely it becomes that you will be controlled and manipulated by unclean spirits. You must remember that you are the righteousness of God in Christ Jesus and an heir to an eternal promise. As the righteousness of God, you choose to live a life free from the bondage of sin.

As you walk in righteousness, you live a life in accordance with God's divine, moral principles. When you walk in righteousness, the Spirit of God overshadows you with uncommon favor and you begin to experience the life that God desires you to have.

SCRIPTURES FOR DELIVERANCE

OVERCOMING FRUSTRATION

1 Peter 5:7 (KJV)
Casting all your care upon him, for he careth for you.

Matthew 11:28 (KJV
Come unto me, all ye that labour and are heavy laden, and I will give you rest

1 Peter 5:7 (AMP)
Casting all your care upon Him, for He cares for you.

Matthew 11:28 (AMP)
Come to Me, all you who labor and are heavy laden, and I will give you rest.

OVERCOMING ANGER

Ephesians 4:26 (KJV)
Be ye angry, and sin not: let not the sun go down upon your wrath:

Romans 12:19 (KJV)

Dearly beloved, avenge not yourselves, but rather give place unto wrath: for it is written, Vengeance is mine; I will repay, saith the Lord

Ephesians 4:26 (AMP)

When angry, do not sin; do not ever let your wrath (your exasperation, your fury or indignation) last until the sun goes down.

Romans 12:19 (AMP)

Beloved, never avenge yourselves, but leave the way one for [God's] wrath; for it is written, Vengeance is Mine, I will repay (requite), says the Lord.

OVERCOMING JEALOUSY

Luke 12:15 (KJV)

And he said unto them, Take heed, and beware of covetousness: for a man's life consisteth not in the abundance of the things which he possesseth.

Proverbs 14:30 (KJV)

A sound heart is the life of the flesh: but envy the rottenness of the bones.

Luke 12:15 (AMP)

And He said to them, Guard yourselves and keep free from all covetousness (the immoderate desire for wealth, the greedy longing to have more); for a man's life does not consist in and is not derived from possessing overflowing abundance or that which is over and above his needs.

Proverbs 14:30 (AMP)
A calm and undisturbed mind *and* heart are the life *and* health of the body, but envy, jealousy, *and*, wrath are like rottenness of the bones.

OVERCOMING RAGE

Proverbs 15:1 (KJV)
A soft answer turns away wrath: but grievous words stir up anger.

Proverbs 14:17 (KJV)
He that is soon angry death foolishly: and a man of wicked devices is hated.

Proverbs 15:1 (AMP)
A SOFT answer turns away wrath, but grievous words stir up anger.

Proverbs 14:17 (AMP)
He who foams up quickly *and* flies into a passion deals foolishly, and a man of wicked plots *and* plans is hated.

OVERCOMING TEMPTATION

1 John 4:4 (KJV)

Ye are of God, little children, and have overcome them: because greater is he that is in you, than he that is in the world.

1 Corinthians 10:13 (KJV)

There hath no temptation taken you but such as is common to man: but God is faithful, who will not suffer you to be tempted above that ye are able; but will with the temptation also make a way to escape, that ye may be able to bear it.

1 John 4:4 (AMP)

Little children, you are of God [you belong to Him] and have [already] defeated *and* overcome them [the agents of the antichrist], because He Who lives in you is greater (mightier) than he who is in the world.

1 Corinthians 10:13 (AMP)

For no temptation, [no matter how it comes or where it leads] has overtaken you *and* laid hold on you that is not common to man [that is, no temptation or trial has come to you that is beyond human resistance *and* that is not adjusted *and* adapted *and* belonging to human experience, and such as man can bear]. But God is faithful, and He [can be trusted] not to let you be tempted beyond your ability *and* strength of resistance *and* power to endure, but with temptation He will [always] provide the way out (the means of escape to a landing place), that you may be capable *and* strong *and* powerful to bear up under it patiently.

OVERCOMING HURT

Psalms 34:18 (KJV)
The Lord is nigh unto them that are of a broken heart; and saveth such as be of a contrite spirit.

2 Timothy 2:1 (KJV)
Thou therefore, my son, be strong in the grace that is in Christ Jesus.

Psalms 34:18 (AMP)
The Lord is near to the heartbroken
And He saves those who are crushed in spirit
(contrite in heart, truly sorry for their sin).

2 Timothy 2:1 (AMP)
So you, my son, be strong [constantly strengthened] *and* empowered in the grace that is [to be found only] in Christ Jesus.

OVERCOMING FEAR

1 Timothy 1:7 (KJV)
For God hath not given us the spirit of fear; but of power, and of love, and of a sound mind.

Psalm 23:4 (KJV)
Yea, though I walk through the valley of the shadow of death, I will fear no evil: for thou art with me; thy rod and thy staff they comfort me.

1 Timothy 1:7 (AMP)

For God did not give us a spirit of timidity *or* cowardice *or* fear, but of power and of love and of sound judgment *and* personal discipline [abilities that result in a calm, well-balanced mind and self-control].

Psalm 23:4 (AMP)

Even though I walk through the [sunless] valley of the shadow of death,
I fear no evil, for You are with me;
Your rod [to protect] and Your staff [to guide], they comfort *and* console me.

OVERCOMING ANXIETY

Philippians 4:6-7 (KJV)

6 Be careful for nothing; but in every thing by prayer and supplication with thanksgiving let your requests be made known unto God.

7 And the peace of God, which passeth all understanding, shall keep your hearts and minds through Christ Jesus.

Philippians 4:6-7 (AMP)

6 Be careful for nothing; but in every thing by prayer and supplication with thanksgiving let your requests be made known unto God.

7 And the peace of God, which passeth all understanding, shall keep your hearts and minds through Christ Jesus.

OVERCOMING LOW SELF-ESTEEM

Psalms 134:14 (KJV)
I will praise thee; for I am fearfully and wonderfully made: marvellous are thy works; and that my soul knoweth right well.

Philippians 4:13 (KJV)
I can do all things through Christ which strengtheneth me.

Psalms 134:14 (KJV)
I will give thanks *and* praise to You, for I am fearfully and wonderfully made;
Wonderful are Your works,
And my soul knows it very well.

Philippians 4:13 (AMP)
I can do all things [which He has called me to do] through Him who strengthens *and* empowers me [to fulfill His purpose—I am self-sufficient in Christ's sufficiency; I am ready for anything and equal to anything through Him who infuses me with inner strength and confident peace.]

OVERCOMING REJECTION

Isaiah 41:10 (KJV)
Fear thou not; for I am with thee: be not dismayed; for I am thy God: I will strengthen thee; yea, I will help thee; yea, I will uphold thee with the right hand of my righteousness.

Jeremiah 29:11 (KJV)
For I know the thoughts that I think toward you, saith the Lord, thoughts of peace, and not of evil, to give you an expected end.

Isaiah 41:10 (AMP)
Do not fear [anything], for I am with you;
Do not be afraid, for I am your God.
I will strengthen you, be assured I will help you;
I will certainly take hold of you with My righteous right hand [a hand of justice, of power, of victory, of salvation].

Jeremiah 29:11 (KJV)
For I know the plans *and* thoughts that I have for you,' says the Lord, 'plans for peace *and* well-being and not for disaster, to give you a future and a hope

OVERCOMING GRIEF

Romans 8:28 (KJV)
And we know that all things work together for good to them that love God, to them who are the called according to his purpose.

Matthew 5:4 (KJV)
Blessed are they that mourn: for they shall be comforted.

Romans 8:28 (AMP)
And we know that God [who is deeply concerned about us] causes all things to work together for good for those who love God, to those who are called according to His plan *and* purpose.

Matthew 5:4 (AMP)
"Blessed [forgiven by God's grace] are those who mourn [over their sins and repent], for they will be comforted [when the burden of sin is lifted]Jesus.

OVERCOMING DISCOURAGEMENT

Deuteronomy 31:6 (KJV)
Be strong and of a good courage, fear not, nor be afraid of them: for the LORD thy God, he it is that doth go with thee; he will not fail thee, nor forsake thee.

Hebrews 4:16 (KJV)

Let us therefore come boldly unto the throne of grace, that we may obtain mercy, and find grace to help in time of need.

Deuteronomy 31:6 (KJV)

Be strong and courageous, do not be afraid or tremble in dread before them, for it is the Lord your God who goes with you. He will not fail you or abandon you."

Hebrews 4:16 (AMP)

Therefore let us [with privilege] approach the throne of grace [that is, the throne of God's gracious favor] with confidence *and* without fear, so that we may receive mercy [for our failures] and find [His amazing] grace to help in time of need [an appropriate blessing, coming just at the right moment].

OVERCOMING ABUSE

Psalm 34:18 (KJV)

The LORD is near to those who have a broken heart, and saves such as have a contrite spirit.

Psalm 82:3 (KJV)

Give justice to the weak and the fatherless; maintain the right of the afflicted and the destitute.

Psalm 107:20 (KJV)
He sent His word and healed them, and delivered them from their destructions.

Psalm 145:14 (KJV)
The LORD upholds all who fall, and raises up all who are bowed down.

Psalm 147:3 (KJV)
He heals the brokenhearted and binds up their wounds.

OVERCOMING ADDICTION

1 Peter 5:10 (KJV)
But the God of all grace, who hath called us unto his eternal glory by Christ Jesus, after that ye have suffered a while, make you perfect, stablish, strengthen, settle [you].

James 4:7 (KJV)
Submit yourselves therefore to God. Resist the devil, and he will flee from you.

1 Corinthians 6:12 (KJV)
All things are lawful unto me, but all things are not expedient: all things are lawful for me, but I will not be brought under the power of any.

Proverbs 20:1 (KJV)

Wine [is] a mocker, strong drink [is] raging: and whosoever is deceived thereby is not wise.

Psalms 50:15 (KJV)

And call upon me in the day of trouble: I will deliver thee, and thou shalt glorify me.

Romans 13:14 (KJV)

But put ye on the Lord Jesus Christ, and make not provision for the flesh, to [fulfil] the lusts [thereof].

INDEX

PROPHETESS DR. MATTIE NOTTAGE BA, MA, DD MINISTRY PROFILE

Widely endorsed as a prophet to the nations, God has used Dr. Mattie Nottage to captivate audiences around the world through her insightful, life-changing messages. Dr. Nottage is married to Apostle Edison Nottage. She co-pastors, along with her husband, Believers Faith Outreach Ministries, International in Nassau, Bahamas.

Mantled with an uncanny spiritual gift of discernment and an undeniable prophetic anointing, Dr. Nottage is a well- respected international preacher, prolific teacher, motivational speaker, life coach, playwright, author, gospel recording artist and revivalist. She is the President and Founder of *Mattie Nottage Ministries, International, The Global Dominion Network Empowering Group of Companies, The Youth In Action Group and The Faith Village For Girls Transformation Program. She is also The Chancellor of The Mattie Nottage School of Ministry. She is the Founder of the prestigious Mattie Nottage Outstanding Kingdom Woman's Award.*

Dr. Nottage has ministered the gospel, in places such as: Ireland, Brazil, Africa, The Netherlands, throughout the United States of America and The Caribbean. Gifted with an authentic anointing, God uses her to "set the captive free" and to fan the flames of revival throughout the nations. Dr. Mattie Nottage, has an endearing passion to train and equip individuals to advance the Kingdom of God and walk in total victory.

She is the author of her bestselling books, ***Breaking The Chains From Worship to Warfare,***

I Refuse To Die, and "Secrets Every Mother Should Tell Her Daughter About Life" Book & Journal. Dr. Nottage is also a regular columnist in The Tribune, the national newspaper of the Bahamas. She has also written numerous publications, stage plays and songs, including the #1 smash hit CD Singles, *"I Refuse To Die In This Place!", "The Verdict Is In...Not Guilty!"* and *"I Still Want You!"*

She has regularly appeared as a guest on various television networks including The Trinity Broadcasting Network (TBN), The Word Network, The Atlanta Live TV and The Babbie Mason Talk Show "Babbie's House" amongst others. Additionally, Dr. Mattie Nottage has been featured in several magazine publications such as the Preaching Woman Magazine and the "Gospel Today" Magazine as one of America's most influential pastors. She, along with her husband, Apostle Edison are the hosts of their very own television show, "Transforming Lives" which airs weekly on The Impact Network.

Dr. Nottage is the former Chairman of the National Youth Advisory Council to the government of the Bahamas and was also recognized and awarded a *"Proclamation of State" by the Mayor and Commissioner of Miami-Dade County, Florida* for her exemplary community initiatives that bring transformation and empowerment to the lives of youth and families globally.

Further, Dr. Nottage has earned her, Bachelor of Arts degree in Christian Counseling, a Masters of Arts degree in Christian Education, and a Doctor of Divinity degree from the renown St. Thomas University, in Jacksonville, Florida and is also a graduate of Kingdom University. Additionally, she has earned her Certified Life Coaching Degree from the F. W. I. Life Coach Training Institute. Dr. Mattie Nottage is known as a Trailblazer and a *"Doctor of Deliverance"* who is committed and dedicated to *Breaking Chains and Transforming Lives*!

PRODUCTS

To request Dr. Mattie Nottage for a speaking engagement, upcoming event, life coaching seminar, mentorship session or to place an order for products, please contact:

Mattie Nottage Ministries, International
(Bahamas Address)

P.O. Box SB-52524 Nassau, N. P. Bahamas

*Tel/Fax: (242) 698-1383 or **(954) 237-8196***

OR

Mattie Nottage Ministries, International
(U.S. Address)

6511 Nova Dr., Suite #193

Davie, Florida 33317

*Tel/Fax: **(888) 825-7568***

UK Tel: 44 (0)203371 9922

FOLLOW US ON:

@DrMattieNottage

Made in the USA
Columbia, SC
13 April 2019